Every Day Is Another Chance

We wish to thank Susan Polis Schutz for permission to reprint the following poems in this publication: "You cannot listen to what others...," "Best friends always remember so well...," "Sing a poem...," and "Nature is the most peaceful...." Copyright © 1983, 1986, 2000, 2004 by Stephen Schutz and Susan Polis Schutz. And for "We need to feel more...." Copyright © 1972 by Continental Publications. Renewed © 2000 by Stephen Schutz and Susan Polis Schutz. And PrimaDonna Entertainment Corp. for "Take time each day to look..." by Donna Fargo. Copyright © 2011 by PrimaDonna Entertainment Corp. And Jason Blume for "Let your goals guide you...." Copyright © 2012 by Jason Blume. And Natasha Josefowitz for "Go where the heart longs to go." Copyright © 1996 by Natasha Josefowitz. All rights reserved.

Library of Congress Control Number: 2013943603
ISBN: 978-1-59842-754-7

▉ and Blue Mountain Press are registered in U.S. Patent and Trademark Office.
Certain trademarks are used under license.

Printed in China.
Second Printing: 2014

Blue Mountain Arts, Inc.
P.O. Box 4549, Boulder, Colorado 80306

Every Day
Is Another
Chance

Simply Positive Ways to
Bring Happiness to Your Life

Edited by Patricia Wayant

Blue Mountain Press™
Boulder, Colorado

Every day is another chance to...

Every day is another chance to…

Shine in Your Own Special Way

No one else in this entire world is exactly like you. You're a one-of-a-kind treasure, uniquely here in this space and time. You are here to shine in your own wonderful way, sharing your smile in the best way you can, and remembering all the while that a little light somewhere makes a brighter light everywhere. You can — and you do — make a wonderful contribution to this world.

Never forget what a treasure you are. You may not always get to hear all the compliments you so sweetly deserve, but you are so worthy of such an abundance… of friendship, joy, and love.

— Douglas Pagels

Every day is another chance to...

Reflect on What's Important

Take time each day to look at your life with thankfulness and as a gift to enjoy.

Look back on your past with an attitude of appreciation for all the lessons that you've learned and a sense of gratitude as you remember every experience. Don't let regrets trouble you and try to steal your joy, for even less-than-positive experiences teach us lessons and help to shape who we are.

Look to the future and know that for every question not yet answered and every dream not yet realized, there is a tomorrow that will hold you gently in its arms and create the perfect way to make your dreams come true.

And for the rest of your life, know that with love, acceptance, peace, and satisfaction, you will reach every goal you set for yourself and do all the things that you want to do.

— Donna Fargo

Every day is another chance to...

Believe in Yourself

Believe in yourself
as others believe in you.
Trust in your strengths
as others trust in them.

Look in the mirror
and see what others see —
a talented, uplifting,
and magnificent person
who can do anything.

Believe in your heart
that you have the power
to grab hold of your future
and mold it into the things
you have always dreamed of.

Trust in your soul
that you are capable of doing
all that needs to be done.

Know that you are
incredible in every way
and see yourself
as others see you...
as an intelligent
and spectacular person.

— Lamisha Serf

Every day is another chance to...

Tell Someone You Love Them

Too many times it seems we take for granted the ones we love. We wait for birthdays or holidays or some other special occasion to say "I love you," "I appreciate you," or "Thank you." We let life carry us away on a never-ending road filled with the responsibilities of a day-to-day existence.

In our busy lives, we often forget that there is more along the way than just bills to pay, phone calls to return, and errands to run. There are people in our lives who need to be hugged, who need to be loved. There are people in our lives who need their accomplishments noticed and praised.

We need to remember how fragile hearts
can be, how quickly a soul can grow weary,
how fast a spirit can break.

We must not forget that a heart is like
a garden that needs to be tended to
and nourished with what only another
heart can give — love and appreciation,
devotion and honesty.

— Tracia Gloudemans

Every day is another chance to...

Give Your Dreams
a Chance

Let your goals guide you
  to the life you are meant to live.
Let your desires remind you to honor
  the gifts and talents you've been
    blessed with.
Let every challenge strengthen your resolve
  to achieve all that you were born to do.

Listen to that voice in your heart
that tells you to take one more step —
even when the road is rough.
Live each and every day to its fullest,
and let the one-of-a-kind
person you are shine through.
Share your gifts with the world,
and live your dreams.

— Jason Blume

Every day is another chance to...

Be Someone
Others Look Up To

Be someone others admire
for the life that you lead and
the kindness that is such a
sweet and natural part of you...

for the way you treat other people...

for how easily a smile finds its way
to your face...

for the work that you do and the
places your journeys take you...

for your dedication to all the right
things and your devotion to
your family...

for how completely you care and
how willingly you are always there
for the people who need you...

for being the light that you are...
in the lives of others.

— L. N. Mallory

Every day is another chance to...

Say "Thank You" and Really Mean It!

"Thank you" is one of those wonderful phrases
people use to express a special gratitude.
But there's often a lot more to it
than those two words can say.

When it comes from the heart,
from deep inside the nicest feelings
and the most special thoughts,
"thank you" means so much.

It means thank you for taking the time
to show that you care.
It means "you really made my day,"
and sometimes it means that you really
make all the days so much better.

It means you make me feel so nice,
   and I wish I could do the same for you...
just by letting you know how much
   you mean to me.

"Thank you" means you didn't have to...
   but I'm so grateful that you did.
"Thank you" means that you've done
   something special that I'll never forget.
                              — Chris Gallatin

Every day is another chance to...

Listen to Your Heart

You cannot listen
to what others
want you to do
You must listen
to yourself
Society
family
friends
and loved ones
do not know what
you must do
Only you know
and only you
can do what is
right for you
— Susan Polis Schutz

Go where the heart
longs to go
Don't pay attention to the feet
that want to stay rooted

Go where the mind
wants to explore
Don't worry about the hands
that still want to hold on

Go where your gut
is fearful to go
Don't let your body
sit in one place

Go where your heart
knows it should go
— Natasha Josefowitz

Every day is another chance to...

Enjoy Life's Little Blessings...

Smiles and joy... the kind that make your heart happy and full.

Peace... a comfort and a quiet within to help you walk your way through each day.

Some mystery and surprises... for they spice up and brighten our lives.

Courage... to handle those days that, for whatever reason, seem more complicated and harder to get through.

Hope... that you'll always realize there is a rainbow waiting at the end of every tunnel.

And love... for nothing else enables the heart to feel treasured or fills the soul with the promise that you matter to others.

— Betsy Bertram

Every day is another chance to...

Be Grateful for What You Have

Be thankful that you don't already have
  everything you desire.
If you did, what would there be to look forward to?
Be thankful when you don't know something,
for it gives you the opportunity to learn.
Be thankful for the difficult times.
During those times, you grow.
Be thankful for your limitations,
because they give you opportunities for
  improvement.

Be thankful for each new challenge,
because it will build your strength and character.
Be thankful for your mistakes.
They will teach you valuable lessons.
Be thankful when you're tired and weary,
because it means you've made an effort.
It's easy to be thankful for the good things.
A life of rich fulfillment comes to those who
    are also thankful for the setbacks.
Gratitude can turn a negative into a positive.
Find a way to be thankful for your troubles,
and they can become your blessings.
                              — Author Unknown

Every day is another chance to...

Keep a Positive Attitude

We cannot choose how many years we
will live, but we can choose how much life
those years will have. We cannot control
the beauty of our face, but we can
control the expression on it. We cannot
control life's difficult moments, but we
can choose to make life less difficult. We
cannot control the negative atmosphere
of the world, but we can control the
atmosphere of our minds. Too often
we try to choose and control things we
cannot. Too seldom we choose to control
what we can... our attitude.

— Author Unknown

I am convinced that attitude is the key to success or failure in almost any of life's endeavors. Your attitude — your perspective, your outlook, how you feel about yourself, how you feel about other people — determines your priorities, your actions, your values. Your attitude determines how you interact with other people and how you interact with yourself.

— Caroline Warner

Every day is another chance to...

Be More Understanding

We need to feel more
to understand others
We need to love more
to be loved back
We need to cry more
to cleanse ourselves
We need to laugh more
to enjoy ourselves

We need to be honest and fair
when interacting with people
We need to establish a strong ethical basis
as a way of life
We need to see more
than our own fantasies
We need to hear more
and listen to the needs of others

We need to give more
and take less
We need to share more
and own less
We need to realize the importance
    of the family
as a backbone to stability
We need to look more
and realize that we are not so
    different from one another

We need to create a world where
we can trust one another
We need to create a world where
we can all peacefully live
the life we choose
                    — Susan Polis Schutz

Every day is another chance to...

Let Go of the Past

Let go...
   of guilt; it's okay to make the same
   mistakes again.
Let go...
   of obsessions; they seldom
   turn out the way you planned.
Let go...
   of hate; it's a waste of love.
Let go...
   of blaming others; you are responsible
   for your own destiny.

Let go...
  of fantasies; give reality a chance to
  come true.
Let go...
  of self-pity; someone else may need you.
Let go...
  of wanting; cherish what you have.
Let go...
  of fear; it's a waste of faith.
Let go...
  of despair; change comes from acceptance
  and forgiveness.
Let go...
  of the past; the future is here —
  right now.
— Kathleen O'Brien

Every day is another chance to...

Begin Again

One of the best things we can do in our lives is this: begin again.

Begin to see yourself as you were when you were the happiest and strongest you've ever been.

Begin to remember what worked for you (and what worked against you), and try to capture the magic again.

Begin to remember how natural it was when you were a child — to live a lifetime each day.

Begin to forget the baggage you have carried with you for years: the problems that don't matter anymore, the tears that cried themselves away, and the worries that are going to wash away on the shore of tomorrow's new beginning.

Every day of your life will be blessed with a brand-new day to follow, and every tomorrow is a time for opportunities to come along and new choices to be made. Be thankful for that fresh start and hopeful about all those possibilities! Turn away from any problems of the past and give the future — and yourself — a chance to become the best of friends.

Sometimes all it takes is a wish in the heart
    to let yourself... begin again.
                                    — Collin McCarty

Every day is another chance to...

Love Yourself

Make a list of things about yourself that you like, and keep it near you at all times so you will always remember your talents and how much you have to offer the world.

⸺

Do your very best to understand what you've got: the wonderful power of your own heart, soul, and hands... which is much, much more than a lot.

— Ashley Rice

Don't ever downplay your abilities or your special charm. Keep living your life the best way you know how — with persistence, patience, and determination. Let go of the bad things and keep the good.

Take time to rediscover yourself. Picture what you want to come into your life. Choose happiness and keep believing in your bright and shining future.

— Vickie M. Worsham

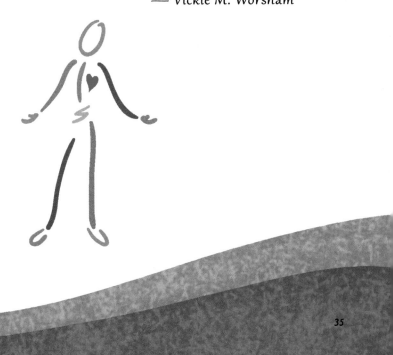

Every day is another chance to...

Find Some Magic

Whether you're sixteen or sixty, I encourage you to have the courage to find the magic in every day. Go out of your way to appreciate the deserving things here before you: people who matter, places that will inevitably change, and circumstances that get rearranged all too easily.

Do more than stop and smell the roses. Search them out. Plant new ones in the places you pass by! Send bouquets of flowers to the people you care about. Remember that there's more to appreciate in this moment than we realize...

Years from now, the truth of this will shine. And one of your sincere regrets will be not knowing how good you had it... at the time.

— Douglas Pagels

Every morning, wake with the awe
   of just being alive.
Each day, discover the magnificent,
   awesome beauty in the world.
Explore and embrace life in yourself
   and in everything you see.
Live every day well.
Let a little sunshine out as well as in.
Create your own rainbows.
Be open to possibilities.
Believe in magic!

— Vickie M. Worsham

Every day is another chance to...

Keep Moving Forward

Don't focus on what was.
Look forward to what can be,
and then do all you can to make it a reality.
Life is what you make of it,
and the challenges that come your way
are just opportunities to right what is wrong.
Don't get discouraged, and don't give up.
You have it all inside yourself,
and you can overcome anything
if you put your mind to it.

— Paula Michele Adams

Constant, slow movement teaches us to keep working like a small creek that stays clear, that doesn't stagnate, but finds a way through numerous details, deliberately.

— Rumi

The great thing in this world is not so much where we are, but in what direction we are moving.

— Oliver Wendell Holmes

Every day is another chance to...

Make Today as Sweet as It Can Be

We cannot change yesterday,
that is quite clear;
nor begin on tomorrow
until it is here.
So all that is left
for you and for me
is to make today
as sweet as can be.

— Author Unknown

Today you have been given this gift: twenty-four hours to spend in the most beautiful and meaningful way possible. Let this day be a reflection of the strength that resides within you; of the courage that lights your path; of the wisdom that guides your steps; and of the serenity that will be yours when this day is done.

This one day, this moment... is your day to shine.

You will live life well — with a happy soul, with a knowing heart, and with an understanding of all they signify — if you remember to live life... one day at a time.

— Jordan Carrill

Every day is another chance to...

Be Brave

You gain strength, courage, and confidence by every experience in which you really stop to look fear in the face. You are able to say to yourself, "I have lived through this... I can take the next thing that comes along."

You must do the thing you think you cannot do.

— Eleanor Roosevelt

You don't have to have all the answers
or always know the right thing to say.
You can climb the highest mountain if
you want... or quietly imagine that you
might someday. You can take chances or
take safety nets, make miracles or make
mistakes. You don't have to be composed
at all hours to be strong. You don't have to
be bold or certain to be brave.

— Ashley Rice

Every day is another chance to...

Stop Procrastinating

Don't put off living until tomorrow.
Don't be afraid to dream some time away.
Don't look too far ahead,
    don't look back with regret;
        just look with hope
            to the horizon of today.

Don't be afraid to reach for your goal,
    no matter how distant it might seem.
And don't be surprised if you succeed.

The truly special people in this world,
    the ones who reach their dreams,
  are the ones who do the things
      they really want to do.

Don't be one of the many...
    be one of the few.

— Collin McCarty

Every day is another chance to...

Release Your Fears

It's okay to be afraid
of the things you don't understand.
It's okay to feel anxious
when things aren't working your way.
It's okay to feel lonely...
even when you're with other people.
It's okay to feel unfulfilled
because you know something is missing
(even if you're not sure what it is).
It's okay to think and worry and cry.

It's okay to do
whatever you have to do,
but just remember, too,
that eventually you're going to adjust
to the changes life brings your way,
and you'll get to the point where
the life you live is full and
satisfying and good to you...
and it will be that way
because you made it that way.

— Laine Parsons

Every day is another chance to...

Take Comfort in Your Faith

Faith isn't anything you can see;
it isn't anything you can touch.
But you can feel it in your heart.
Faith is what keeps you trying
when others would have given up.

Faith is trusting in a power
greater than yourself
and knowing that whatever happens,
this power will carry you through anything.
It is believing in yourself
and having the courage
to stand up for what you believe in.

Faith is peace in the midst of a storm,
determination in the midst of adversity,
and safety in the midst of trouble.
For nothing can touch a soul
that is protected by faith.

— Barbara Cage

Every day is another chance to...

Sing, Dance, and Have Fun

You don't have to know <u>how</u> to sing.
It's feeling as though you <u>want</u> to
that makes the day worthwhile.
> — Coleman Cox

Sing a song
Read a poem
Paint a picture
Dance to the music in your head
Rise up
and touch the stars —
today
> — Susan Polis Schutz

Spend a while in the garden or the park or the path amongst the trees. Do the things that please you, as well as the things you have to do. Fulfill the work and the tasks of the day while discovering something new and different along the way. Grow, learn, reach out. Be curious. Be childlike.

Remember what imagination is all about. Share a smile, a feeling, a certain personal thought from the heart, from the soul. Care. Kick off your shoes. Sing along with your song. Be less concerned about what others think of you. Be more accepting of the very special person who lives inside you.

— Collin McCarty

Every day is another chance to...

Be a Winner

Winners take chances.
Like everyone else, they fear failing,
but they refuse to let fear control them.
Winners don't give up.
When life gets rough, they hang in
until the going gets better.
Winners are flexible.
They realize there is more than one way
and are willing to try others.
Winners know they are not perfect.
They respect their weaknesses
while making the most of their strengths.
Winners fall, but they don't stay down.
They stubbornly refuse to let a fall
    keep them from climbing.

Winners don't blame
   fate for their failures
or luck for their successes.
Winners accept responsibility
   for their lives.
Winners are positive thinkers
   who see good in all things.
From the ordinary, they make
   the extraordinary.
Winners believe in the path they
   have chosen
even when it's hard,
even when others can't see
   where they are going.
Winners are patient.
They know a goal is only as worthy
as the effort that's required
   to achieve it.

— Nancye Sims

Think Big

Look into your heart, search your dreams,
and be honest about what you really want;
then do whatever it takes to get it.

Live like you mean it. Believe you can...
and you will!

— Barbara Cage

Don't put limits on yourself.
So many dreams are waiting to be realized.
Decisions are too important to leave to chance.
Reach for your peak, your goal, your prize.

Realize that it's never too late.
Do ordinary things in an extraordinary way.
Have health and hope and happiness.
Take the time to wish upon a star.

— Collin McCarty

Say "yes" to challenges, and dare to make
those big, bold dreams come true.

— Jacqueline Schiff

Every day is another chance to...

Make Time for Yourself

At any given moment on any given day, you are needed. Needed to talk... to drive... to sing... to dance... to laugh... to listen... to help... to walk... to do... something. You say you'll make time for yourself when things slow down, but things will never slow down unless you allow them to.

There will always be that something waving in the background relentlessly trying to get your attention. It's up to you to turn your back... shut your eyes... walk in the opposite direction of that something that just refuses to give you a break. Take the time you deserve to check in with yourself and see what you need for a change.

Be completely and utterly selfish, and do not let guilt creep into your sacred space. No, it's not easy, which is why you have to commit to making a conscious effort to concentrate solely on yourself and your needs. Say no. Unplug your phone. Lock your door to the world. Do whatever it takes to make yourself the ultimate priority.

— Elle Mastro

Every day is another chance to...

Never Give Up Hope

Hope is a beautiful answer to many difficult questions. Hope only asks that you believe. Hope only wants you to receive. Hope is "hanging in there" until help arrives. Whenever a day didn't go as planned, hope is there as a comforting guide to help you understand.

Hope is a quiet, personal place where you can always take shelter. Hope is the warm and welcomed knowledge that beautiful possibilities exist. Hope is all these special things, and in simply knowing this:

When hope is all you've got...
   you still have got a lot.

           — Collin McCarty

As long as we have hope, we have direction, the energy to move, and the map to move by. We have a hundred alternatives, a thousand paths, and an infinity of dreams. Hopeful, we are halfway to where we want to go.

— Author Unknown

Be like the bird
That, pausing in her flight
Awhile on boughs too slight,
Feels them give way
Beneath her and yet sings,
Knowing that she hath wings.

— Victor Hugo

Every day is another chance to...

Have a Friend...
Be a Friend

A friend is one of the nicest things you can have, and one of the best things you can be. A friend is a living treasure, and if you have one, you have one of the most valuable gifts in life.

A friend is the one who will always be beside you, through all the laughter and through each and every tear. A friend is the one thing you can always rely on; the someone you can always open up to; the one wonderful person who always believes in you in a way that no one else seems to.

A friend is a sanctuary. A friend is a smile.

A friend is a hand that is always holding yours, no matter where you are, no matter how close or far apart you may be. A friend is someone who is always there and will always — always — care. A friend is a feeling of forever in the heart.

A friend is the one door that is always open. A friend is the one to whom you can give your key. A friend is one of the nicest things you can have... and one of the best things you can be.

— Douglas Pagels

Every day is another chance to...

Let Love Be Your Guide

Love illumines the mind, gives new life to every fiber in your being, removes almost every burden, and eases the whole path of existence. Love removes entirely all anger, hatred, revenge, ill will, and similar states — a matter of great importance, for no one can live an ideal life while such states of mind remain.... The person who loves everybody with that larger loving kindness has taken a long step upward into that life that is real life. This is not mere sentiment, but the expression of an exact scientific fact. A strong, continuous love will bring all good to anyone who lives and acts as he inwardly feels.

— Christian D. Larson

Love all God's creation,
the whole and every
grain of sand in it. Love every
leaf, every ray of God's light.
Love the animals, love the plants,
love everything. If you love
everything, you will perceive the
divine mystery in things. Once
you perceive it, you will begin to
comprehend it better every day. And
you will come at last to love the whole
world with an all-embracing love.

— Fyodor Dostoyevsky

Love is something eternal — the aspect may
change, but not the essence. There is the same
difference in a person before and after he is in
love as there is in an unlighted lamp and one
that is burning. The lamp was there and it was a
good lamp, but now it is shedding light, too, and
that is its real function.

— Vincent van Gogh

Every day is another chance to...

Change the World

Be someone who brings sunshine
when skies are gray,
someone who laughs
so much along the way.
Someone who sparkles and shines
and makes the world
a better place to be.

— Ashley Rice

When I was a young man, I wanted to change the world. I found it was difficult to change the world, so I tried to change my nation. When I found I couldn't change the nation, I began to focus on my town. I couldn't change the town and as an older man, I tried to change my family.

Now, as an old man, I realize the only thing I can change is myself, and suddenly I realize that if long ago I had changed myself, I could have made an impact on my family. My family and I could have made an impact on our town. Their impact could have changed the nation, and I could, indeed, have changed the world.

— Unknown Monk, AD 1100

Every day is another chance to...

Practice Acceptance and Forgiveness

Forgiveness is letting go of the pain
and accepting what has happened,
because it will not change.

It is dismissing the blame.
Choices were made that caused the hurt;
you each could have chosen differently,
but you didn't.

Forgiveness is starting over with
the knowledge that you have gained.

— Judith Mammay

If you can forgive
yourself as well as
others, and if you can
learn from your mistakes,
problems and heartaches will be
steppingstones on your path to growing wiser
and stronger.

If you can love yourself as well as others,
you will learn acceptance and understanding.

— Barbara Cage

One of the secrets of a long and fruitful life
is to forgive everybody everything every night
before you go to bed.

— Author Unknown

Every day is another chance to...

Go for It!

Life is not easy for any of us.
But what of that? We must
have perseverance and above
all confidence in ourselves. We
must believe that we are gifted
for something and that this thing
must be attained.
                              — Marie Curie

Don't wait for what you want
    to come to you.
Go after it with all that you are,
knowing that life will meet you halfway.

— Nancye Sims

You will be whatever you resolve to be.
Determine to be something in the world,
    and you will be something.

"I cannot" never accomplished anything.

But "I will try" has worked wonders.

— Joel Hawes

Every day is another chance to...

Exercise Those Smile Muscles

It takes forty-three muscles to frown but only seventeen to smile. So smile — it conserves energy.

— Author Unknown

Real optimism is aware of problems
but recognizes the solutions, knows
about difficulties but believes they can
be overcome, sees the negatives but
accentuates the positives, is exposed to
the worst but expects the best, has reason
to complain but chooses to smile.
— William Arthur Ward

A smile is the light
in the window of your face
that tells people that
your heart is at home.
— Author Unknown

Every day is another chance to...

Find Happiness in Your Work

Few persons realize how much of their happiness is dependent upon their work, upon the fact that they are kept busy and not left to feed upon themselves. Happiness comes most to persons who seek her least, and think least about her. It is not an object to be sought; it is a state to be induced. It must follow and not lead. It must overtake you, and not you overtake it. How important is health to happiness, yet the best promoter of health is something to do.

Blessed is the man who has some congenial work, some occupation in which he can put his heart.

— John Burroughs

Of all the unhappy people in the world, the unhappiest are those who have not found something they want to do. True happiness comes to him who does his work well, followed by a relaxing and refreshing period of rest. True happiness comes from the right amount of work for the day.

— Lin Yutang

Every day is another chance to...

Get Rich

Want to know the real secret of getting rich? It's easy... you just need to remember this:

Friendships are priceless, time is invaluable, health is wealth, and love is a treasure.

Count your blessings. Invest in your dreams. Profit from experience. Share your good fortune.

And spend your hours wisely each day.

Someday we'll all look back at our lives and realize that it's actually kind of funny... discovering that the things we valued most had absolutely nothing to do... with money.

— Douglas Pagels

Every day is another chance to...

Be a Failure

Don't be discouraged by a failure. It can be a positive experience. Failure is, in a sense, the highway to success, inasmuch as every discovery of what is false leads us to seek earnestly after what is true.
— John Keats

Many of life's failures are people who did not realize how close they were to success when they gave up.
— Thomas Alva Edison

Success is not measured by
whether you win or
whether you fail —
there's always a little bit
of success, even if things
don't go your way.
What's important is that you'll
feel better about yourself
for the simple reason
that you tried.

— Amanda Pierce

Watch for Angels

Every day in the world around us, real-life angels are doing the things they do... and bringing more smiles to the world around them. They don't hold things against you; the only thing they hold... is you. They take your hand in theirs when you could use a little reassurance. They walk beside you when you could do with a little guidance and direction in your life. And they support you in your attempts to do what is right.

Real-life angels multiply your smiles and add to your integrity. They make you feel like, "Hey, I really am somebody who matters." Then they quietly prove to you how beautiful and true that feeling really is.

If you come across an angel like this, you are one of the luckiest people of all.

— Emilia Larson

Every day is another chance to...

Welcome Solitude

Settle into yourself
Be truly alone
And not the kind of alone
that makes your heart sore
but the kind that causes
your breath to slow
your limbs to go weightless
your thoughts to fall from you
one by one

Embrace the moment
that leaves you in
complete solitude
Welcome these times
as a gift of peace
for your spirit and soul...

Your sustenance

— Elle Mastro

Every day is another chance to...

Call Your Best Friend

Best friends always
remember so well
all the things they did together
all the subjects they discussed
all the mistakes they made
all the fun they had

Best friends always remember
how their friendship
was such a stabilizing force
during confusing times
in their lives

Best friends may have
different lifestyles
live in different places
and interact with different people
but no matter how much
their lives may change
their friendship remains the same

— Susan Polis Schutz

Every day is another chance to...

Find Pleasure in the Smallest Things

Each day is an opportunity to share our hearts, our love, and our lives to the fullest. Sometimes that means just making the most out of the smallest things — like listening to each other, holding each other's hand, or just being together.

— Star Nakamoto

You don't have to be the one responsible
for making everything work. Believe me.
The big things are already taken care
of: the sun will rise in the morning, the
stars will come out at night, and — if
you work it right — a child, a love, or
a close, dear friend will share a special
smile with you — and make everything
wrong... right again.

— Douglas Pagels

Life is really simple, but we insist
on making it complicated.

— Confucius

Every day is another chance to…

Be in the Moment

If we wait for the moment when
everything, absolutely everything,
is ready, we shall never begin.
— Ivan Turgenev

Just focus on "right now" —
not the future or the past…
just this one moment
right here where you stand.
— Ashley Rice

Live to the fullest, and make each day count. Don't let the important things go unsaid. Have simple pleasures in this complex world. Be a joyous spirit and a sensitive soul. Take those long walks that would love to be taken. Explore those sunlit paths that would love to oblige. Don't just have minutes in the day; have moments in time.

— Douglas Pagels

Every day is another chance to...

Forget Your Troubles

Forget problems
that don't matter anymore
and worries that will wash away
on the shore of tomorrow.
Determine your own worth
by yourself,
and do not be dependent
on another's judgment of you.
Live life fully
with thankfulness and joy
for all the gifts
you've been given.

— Debbi Oehman

Troubles are only mental; it is the
mind that manufactures them, and
the mind can gorge them, banish
them, abolish them.
                — Mark Twain

There are times when life isn't all
you want, but it's all you have.
So what I say is: Have it! Stick a
geranium in your hat and be happy!
                — Author Unknown

Every day is another chance to...

Take It Slow and Easy

Never be in a hurry; do everything quietly and in a calm spirit. Do not lose your inward peace for anything whatsoever, even if your whole world seems upset.

— Francis de Sales

To walk when others are running,
To whisper when others are shouting;
To sleep when others are restless,
To smile when others are angry;
To work when others are idle,
To pause when others are hurrying;
To pray when others are doubting,
To think when others are in confusion;
To face turmoil, yet feel composure;
To know inner calm in spite of
    everything —
This is the test of serenity.

— Doris Lacasse

Every day is another chance to...

Remember When...

We can never lose the memories
that bring happiness to our lives —
the funny stories and special moments
that live to make us laugh again.
We are blessed to have memories;
they are a permanent connection,
a beautiful way to meet again,
and a lifelong link to those we love.

— Barbara J. Hall

No matter where we go in life,
we always remember the special people
who have touched our lives,
who have loved us and helped us
learn more about ourselves,
who have stayed by us
when we had to face difficult times,
and with whom we have felt safe enough
to reveal our true selves.
We always remember the special people
we dreamed and planned
great futures with,
who accepted us as we were
and encouraged us to become
all that we wanted to be.

— Donna Levine-Small

Every day is another chance to...

Be Inspired by Nature

Nature is the most peaceful environment for clarifying your thoughts and putting things into perspective.

— Susan Polis Schutz

When I go into my garden with a spade
and dig a bed, I feel such an exhilaration
and health that I discover that I have been
defrauding myself all this time in letting
others do for me what I should have done
with my own hands.

— Ralph Waldo Emerson

Whenever the pressure of our complex city
life thins my blood and benumbs my brain,
I seek relief in the trail. And when I hear
the coyote wailing to the yellow dawn, my
cares fall from me — I am happy.

— Hamlin Garland

Every day is another chance to...

Take a Walk

A walk. The atmosphere incredibly pure — a warm, caressing gentleness in the sunshine — joy in one's whole being.... Forgotten impressions of childhood and youth came back to me — all those indescribable effects wrought by color, shadow, sunlight, green hedges, and songs of birds, upon the soul just opening to poetry. I became young again, wondering, and simple, as candor and ignorance are simple. I abandoned myself to life and to nature, and they cradled me with an infinite gentleness.

— Henri-Frédéric Amiel

The sum of the whole is this: walk and be happy; walk and be healthy. The best way to lengthen our days is to walk steadily and with a purpose.

— Charles Dickens

Walking is the best possible exercise. Habituate yourself to walk very far.

— Thomas Jefferson

Every day is another chance to...

Appreciate the Things Money Can't Buy

Money may buy the husk of things,
but not the kernel. It brings you food
but not appetite, medicine but not
health, acquaintances but not friends...
days of joy but not peace or happiness.

— Henrik Ibsen

It is not how much we have,
but how much we enjoy,
that makes happiness.

— Charles H. Spurgeon

To be rich in admiration and free from envy; to rejoice greatly in the good of others; to love with such generosity of heart that your love is still a dear possession in absence. These are the gifts of fortune which money cannot buy, and without which money can buy nothing.

— Robert Louis Stevenson

Every day is another chance to...

Try a Little Harder

Someday... you'll see. It will all be worth it. All the hopes, all the dreams. The sacrifices. The courage. All the hard work. All of it will turn out to be abundantly worthwhile.

Someday you'll open the door on a brand-new day and be rewarded with everything working out just the way you wanted it to. So never stop believing in the things you want to come true.

Just start by taking one step in the right direction. Then another. And if you have the faith and the will to continue on, do you know what you'll discover?

How capable you are, how amazing you can be, and how patience and belief can lead to some very meaningful things and some very lasting gifts. — Chris Gallatin

Every day is another chance to...

Give Generously

The best thing to give:
>   to your enemy, forgiveness;
>   to an opponent, tolerance;
>   to a friend, your heart;
>   to a child, a good example;
>   to a father, deference;
>   to your mother, conduct that
>   will make her proud of you;
>   to yourself, respect;
>   to all men, charity.

— Arthur James Balfour

Love is the greatest gift
we can give to one another,
and giving is one of the
greatest joys life bestows
upon us. — Laurie Wymer

It's not what you possess, but
what you do with what you have.
— Thomas Carlyle

Every day is another chance to...

Look for Beauty Everywhere

There is so much beauty all around
you: the beauty of sunrise and sunset;
of star-filled sky and the wonder of its
endlessness; the beauty of flowers, of a
child's smile; the beauty of poetry, prose,
and music. Take time to see it, hear it,
smell it, and be comforted by it! The world
isn't drab — appreciate its marvelous
colors, sounds, and fragrances.

— Paul K. Poulsen

Never lose an opportunity of seeing anything that is beautiful; for beauty is God's handwriting — a wayside sacrament. Welcome it in every fair face, in every fair sky, in every fair flower, and thank God for it as a cup of blessing.

— Ralph Waldo Emerson

Every day is another chance to...

Take Good Care

Care enough about yourself to eat right, get enough exercise and rest, and not do anything that would cause you harm, now or in the future.

Have goals and dreams, and pursue them to the best of your ability. Balance hard work with enough time for fun and socializing too.

Have someone to confide in, laugh with, and explore new things with — someone who enjoys the same activities you do and who is a great listener.

Have an open heart, an open mind, and a bright outlook that allows you to see all sides of a situation and make the best of whatever comes your way.

Have confidence in yourself, your talents, your abilities, and your uniqueness. Believe that you are a likeable and desirable person who deserves respect and consideration.

Let love be something that comes so naturally to you that you give it away, share it, and are always open to receive it.

— Barbara Cage

Every day is another chance to...

Brighten the Lives of Others

Do your part in helping those
    less fortunate,
walk hand in hand with those
    of less talent,
follow those of more knowledge,
and be an equal with those who
    are different.
Find your special purpose in this world
    so full of choices
and help lead those who stray.

— Jackie Olson

Helping our fellow man is the rent for
the space we occupy on this earth —
the more rent you pay, the greater will
be your happiness and joy in living.

— Author Unknown

In big ways, in small ways,
in every single way...
the people who take the time
to go out of their way
to brighten the lives of others
are the ones who deserve
the sweetest thanks of all.

— Rebecca Molson

Every day is another chance to...

Find Your Soul Mate

The sweetest thing that can happen to anyone is to meet that one special person who makes you feel like you're living in a dream come true. It's like that with every smile, every touch, every memory you make.

When almost every day you have together is the kind you don't want to end... that's when you know. That's when love is real, and it's when you realize what a treasure you're holding on to.

— Casey Whilson

Love is the miracle that can take two lives and mold them into one, take two souls and bind them for life, take two hearts and fill them with enough passion and tenderness to last a lifetime.

Love is a blessing that will lead you down life's most beautiful path.

— Michele Weber

Every day is another chance to...

Keep Peace in Your Heart

Here's the thing... life changes a lot.
So cherish the things you love most,
and keep a sharp eye out
for the good in everyday life.
Be aware of pitfalls —
those situations that don't feel quite right —
and keep peace in your heart.

Even when it's raining,
when the world around you
is spinning and flailing,
when the door won't open
and the car won't start —
keep peace in your heart.

— Ashley Rice

Live so that you are at ease, in
harmony with the world, and
full of joy. Day and night, share
the springtime with all things,
thus creating the seasons in your
own heart.

— Confucius

Happiness is when what you
think, what you say, and what
you do are in harmony.

— Mahatma Gandhi

Every day is another chance to...

Be Proud of
Your Accomplishments

In everyone's life
there are moments
of pride and accomplishment
that are remembered forever.

Through the years,
you have set goals and met challenges
with enough courage and determination
to overcome the many obstacles
that you've encountered along the way.

Success is not measured by how well
you fulfill the expectations of others,
but by how honestly you live up to
your own expectations.
When you are true to yourself
in the pursuit of your dreams,
you earn the right to be proud
of your accomplishments.

— Linda Principe

Every day is another chance to...

Say a Prayer, Make a Wish

A prayer, in its simplest definition, is merely a wish turned heavenward.

— Phillips Brooks

Every time you pray, if your prayer is sincere, there will be new feeling and new meaning in it, which will give you fresh courage.

— Fyodor Dostoyevsky

Wish for small pleasures and big joys
and happy skies that always
shine down upon you;
more smiles and laughter
than you have ever had before;
contentment and well-being
that follow you everywhere;
all the things that mean
the world to you;
prayers that soar to heaven
and a guardian angel at your side.
— Linda E. Knight

Every day is another chance to...

Celebrate the Sheer Joy of Being Alive

The days of our lives fly by like the wind,
as if we were swiftly gliding down
a mysterious highway.
We no sooner pass a major landmark
than it seems to vanish
in the rearview mirror.
But sometimes we need
to take stock and reflect,
to pull over, smell the roses,
and see the starlight...
to celebrate everything we have been,
everything we are,
and everything we will be.
— Michael Shevlane

Just to look at the sun going down behind green hills; just to watch rain falling on a quiet lake; just to see spinning tops of sand, created by winds whirling over a desert; just to be able to imagine oneself upon a ship, docking at a pier in a strange and distant port; just to be able to touch the hand of another and feel oneself become a part of that other; just to breathe the evening air and hear the voices of children, raised in laughter; oh, just to feel one is a part of all the scheme of things entire — such are the blessings humans have.

— G. Allison Phelps

Every day is another chance to...

Promise Yourself

Promise yourself
to dream more and hesitate less.
To believe in yourself more
and judge yourself less by
the accomplishments of others.
To accept life as it comes
and truly make each day special.

— Deanna Beisser

Promise to always remember what a special person you are. Promise to hold on to your hopes and reach out for your stars. Promise to live with happiness over the years and over the miles. Promise to "remember when..." and always "look forward to...." Promise to do the things you have always wanted to do. Promise to cherish your dreams as treasures you have kept. Promise to enjoy life day by day and step by step.

— Collin McCarty

Every day is another chance to...

Have a Wonderful Day...
Every Day

May each day come to you wrapped
in all the wonder and joy of living.
May each day be full of memories
and bring you all you're reaching for.
May there always be a thousand wishes
   shining over you.
May each day bring on the fun,
pull out all the stops,
and be one rainbow after another.
May it make your heart sing,
your feet dance, and your wings soar.
May it bring you all the happiness
   you deserve.

May each day come wrapped in love,
tied with joy, and sealed with memories.
May it bring one big surprise after another.
May you take the time to remember
there's no one else like you —
no smile as warm, no hug as gentle,
no friendship as beautiful.
May each day celebrate your strengths,
honor your understanding,
and recognize your goodness.
May each day be wonderful.

— Linda E. Knight

Blue Mountain Arts®

New and Best-Selling Titles

By Susan Polis Schutz:
To My Daughter with Love on the Important Things in Life
To My Son with Love

By Douglas Pagels:
For You, My Soul Mate
Required Reading for All Teenagers
The Next Chapter of Your Life

By Marci:
Friends Are Forever
10 Simple Things to Remember
To My Daughter
To My Mother
To My Sister
You Are My "Once in a Lifetime"

By Wally Amos, with Stu Glauberman:
The Path to Success Is Paved with Positive Thinking

By M. Butler and D. Mastromarino:
Take Time for You

By James Downton, Jr.:
Today, I Will... Words to Inspire Positive Life Changes

By Carol Wiseman:
Emerging from the Heartache of Loss

Anthologies:
A Daughter Is Life's Greatest Gift
A Son Is Life's Greatest Gift
Dream Big, Stay Positive, and Believe in Yourself
God Is Always Watching Over You
Hang In There
Keep Believing in Yourself and Your Dreams
The Love Between a Mother and Daughter Is Forever
The Peace Within You
There Is Nothing Sweeter in Life Than a Granddaughter
Think Positive Thoughts Every Day
When I Say I Love You
Words Every Woman Should Remember